Beautiful Flowers
COLOURING BOOK

ARCTURUS

This edition published in 2021 by Arcturus Publishing Limited
26/27 Bickels Yard, 151–153 Bermondsey Street,
London SE1 3HA

Copyright © Arcturus Holdings Limited

All rights reserved. No part of this publication may be reproduced, stored in a retrieval system, or transmitted, in any form or by any means, electronic, mechanical, photocopying, recording or otherwise, without prior written permission in accordance with the provisions of the Copyright Act 1956 (as amended). Any person or persons who do any unauthorised act in relation to this publication may be liable to criminal prosecution and civil claims for damages.

ISBN: 978-1-83857-602-8
CH004980NT
Supplier 34, Date 1021, Print run 12064

Printed in China

Created for children 10+

Introduction

There is endless interest to be had in depicting the world's flowers, and the delight of a colouring-in book is that you can get straight into applying colours without worrying about your drawing skills. You may decide that your colouring could do with a little refinement next time, but you won't have to worry that your shapes and proportions are so far off course that your subject is hard to recognize.

The plates in this book are drawn from *Choix des Plus Belles Fleurs* (*Choice of the Most Beautiful Flowers*) by Pierre-Joseph Redouté, published in 1827. At one time court artist to Queen Marie Antoinette, Redouté studied botany in depth and illustrated more than 1800 plant species. Today, he remains one of the most famous artists in the genre of botanical painting.

You will probably find that coloured pencils are the easiest tools to use here, blending them to achieve a richly coloured finish and following the natural direction of the subject's textures, working along the lines of the leaves and petals. Alternatively, try watercolour paints. Buy a small boxed set of the best quality that you can afford, and a watercolour brush with a fine point – a No. 6 round brush is a good general size. With these few simple tools, you'll be equipped to have a go at the blooms that Redouté brought to life two centuries ago.

Diana Vowles

Key: *List of plates*

1 Crown imperial, yellow variety (*Fritillaria imperialis*)

2 *Gloxinia* variety

3 *Amaryllis* variety

4 Bunch-flowered narcissus (*Narcissus tazetta*)

5 Japanese camellia (*Camellia japonica*)

6 Tulip (*Tulipa culta*)

7 Common hyacinth (*Hyacinthus orientalis*)

8 Poppy (*Papaver somniferum*)

9 Dutch iris (*Iris × hollandica*)

10 Blanket flower (*Gaillardia*)

11 Snapdragon (*Antirrhinum majus*)

12 Blue false indigo (*Baptisia australis*)

13 Chinese peony (*Paeonia lactiflora*)

14 Winged-stem passion flower (*Passiflora alata*)

15 Knysna lily (*Cyrtanthus obliquus*)

16 Fringed iris (*Iris japonica*)

17 Harlequin flower (*Sparaxis tricolor*)

18 Angel's trumpet (*Datura*)

19 Crown imperial (*Fritillaria imperialis*)

20 Blue Egyptian water lily or blue lotus (*Nymphaea caerulea*)

21 Hanging bells (*Enkianthus quinqueflorus*)

22 *Hippeastrum* variety

23 Lady's-slipper orchid (*Cypripedium calceolus*)

24 Auricula or mountain cowslip (*Primula auricula*)

25 Tulip tree
or Yellow poplar
(*Liriodendron tulipifera*)

26 Blue plantain lily
(*Hosta ventricosa*, formerly
Hemerocallis caerulea)

27 Sulphur rose
(*Rosa hemisphaerica*)

28 Sweet pea
(*Lathyrus odoratus*)

29 Dwarf morning glory
(*Convolvulus tricolor*)

30 Oleander
(*Nerium oleander*)

31 Snake vine
(*Hibbertia scandens*)

32 Heartsease
(*Viola tricolor*)

33 Cabbage rose
(*Rosa* × *centifolia*
'Bullata')

34 Common peony
(*Paeonia officinalis*)

35 Spanish iris
(*Iris xiphium* variety)

36 *Lychnis Coronata*
(syn. *L. grandiflora*)

37 Poppy anemone or Spanish marigold (*Anemone coronaria*)

38 Dahlia (*Dahlia coccinaea*)

39 Dalmation iris (*Iris pallida*)

40 Morning glory (*Ipomoea purpurea*)

41 Fern-leaf peony (*Paeonia tenuifolia*)

42 Nettle-leaved bellflower (*Campanula trachelium*)

43 China aster (*Callistephus chinensis*)

44 Bouquet of camellias, narcissus and pansies

Fritillaria imperialis

Crown imperial, yellow variety

Gloxinia variety

Gloxinia variety

Amaryllis variety

Amaryllis variety

Narcissus tazetta

Bunch-flowered narcissus

Camellia japonica

Japanese camellia

Tulipa culta

Tulip

Hyacinthus orientalis

Common hyacinth

Papaver somniferum

Poppy

Iris × hollandica

Dutch iris

Gaillardia

Blanket flower

Antirrhinum majus

Snapdragon

Baptisia australis

Blue false indigo

Paeonia lactiflora

Chinese peony

Passiflora alata

Winged-stem passion flower

Cyrtanthus obliquus

Knysna lily

Iris japonica

Fringed iris

Sparaxis tricolor

Harlequin flower

Datura

Angel's trumpet

Fritillaria imperialis

Crown imperial

Nymphaea caerulea

Blue Egyptian water lily or blue lotus

Enkianthus quinqueflorus

Hanging bells

Hippeastrum variety

Hippeastrum variety

Cypripedium calceolus

Lady's-slipper orchid

Primula auricula

Auricula or mountain cowslip

Liriodendron tulipifera

Tulip tree or Yellow poplar

Hosta ventricosa, formerly *Hemerocallis caerulea*

Blue plantain lily

Rosa hemisphaerica

Sulphur rose

Lathyrus odoratus

Sweet pea

Convolvulus tricolor

Dwarf morning glory

Nerium oleander

Oleander

Hibbertia scandens

Snake vine

Viola tricolor

Heartsease

Rosa × centifolia 'Bullata'

Cabbage rose

Paeonia officinalis

Common peony

Iris xiphium variety

Spanish iris

Lychnis Coronata

syn. *L. grandiflora*

Anemone coronaria

Poppy anemone or Spanish marigold

Dahlia coccinaea

Dahlia

Iris pallida

Dalmation iris

Ipomoea purpurea

Morning glory

Paeonia tenuifolia

Fern-leaf peony

Campanula trachelium

Nettle-leaved bellflower

Callistephus chinensis

China aster

Bouquet of camellias, narcissus and pansies

Bouquet of camellias, narcissus and pansies